The Civil War

THE MEN WHO FOUGHT
THE CIVIL WAR

Linda R. Wade

ABDO
Daughters Publishing

Visit us at
www.abdopub.com

Published by Abdo Publishing Company, 4940 Viking Drive, Edina, MN 55435.
Copyright ©1998 by Abdo Consulting Group, Inc. International copyrights
reserved in all countries. No part of this book may be reproduced in any form
without written permission from the publisher.

Printed in the United States.

Graphic Design: John Hamilton
Contributing Editors: John Hamilton; Alan Gergen; Elizabeth Clouter-Gergen
Cover photo: John Hamilton; Digital Stock
Interior photos: Digital Stock, pages 1, 5, 6, 8, 9, 10, 12, 15, 16, 21, 26, 28
                  AP/Wide World Photos, page 17
                  National Archives, pages 13, 14, 19, 23, 24, 25, 27, 31

Sources: Morris, Jeffrey, and Morris, Richard. *Encyclopedia of American History*
(7th ed.). New York: Harper, 1996; DeGregorio, William A. *Complete Book of*
U.S. Presidents. New York: Random House, 1997; *Historical Statistics of the*
United States to 1970. U.S. Department of Commerce—Bureau of the Census;
Ward, Geoffrey. *The Civil War*. New York: Knopf, 1991; Jordan, Robert. *The*
Civil War. Washington, D.C.: National Geographic Society, 1969.

Library of Congress Cataloging–in–Publication Data

Wade, Linda R.
    The men who fought the Civil War / Linda R. Wade
        p. cm. — (The Civil War)
    Includes index.
    Summary: Looks at the soldiers and generals who fought in the Civil War,
including both Union and Confederate armies, as well as President Lincoln's
work to end the conflict and abolish slavery.
    ISBN   1-56239-823-7
    1. Soldiers—United States—History—19th century—Juvenile literature.
2. Generals—United States—Biography—Juvenile literature. 3. Soldiers—
Confederate States of America—History—19th century—Juvenile literature.
4. Generals—Confederate States of America—Biography—Juvenile literature.
5. United States. Army—History—Civil War, 1861-1865—Juvenile literature.
6. Confederate States of America. Army—Juvenile literature. [1. United
States—History—Civil War, 1861-1865. 2. Soldiers. 3. Generals.]
I. Title. II. Series: Wade, Linda R. Civil War.
E607.W34 1998
973.7' 3' 0922—dc21   97-37477
                                                 CIP
                                                 AC

CONTENTS

INTRODUCTION

It is hard to imagine thousands of men on the battlefield—each facing death with only a gun and a bayonet for protection. It is difficult to think about sleeping in a tent with only a thin blanket while the wind is blowing wildly all around. It is a sad thought to realize that to be wounded meant agony because there was little or no pain medication.

We often read about Generals Lee and Grant and the big battles of the Civil War, but who were the soldiers out there bravely fighting? And who were the people who helped those brave soldiers?

War was much different in the 1860s than it is today. Medicine for the sick or injured soldier was rare. If an arm or leg was badly damaged, it was cut off.

Few women worked outside of the home in those days. During the war, women had many more responsibilities. How did families survive the changes?

Discover what it was like to be a soldier during the Civil War. Find out about the people who helped the soldiers.

Facing page: A Union soldier bearing the flag of the 8th Pennsylvania Infantry.

CHAPTER 1

THE GENERALS

Ulysses S. Grant was the North's most celebrated commander. He first came to national attention when he captured the Confederate stronghold of Fort Donelson in the early part of 1862. President Lincoln had a lot of faith in Grant, and promoted him to lieutenant general early in 1864. Grant fought against the famous Robert E. Lee in several of the last battles.

In 1868 Grant became president of the United States. He served two terms. He died of throat cancer in 1885.

Robert E. Lee was a man that both sides wanted to recruit. When the Civil War broke out in 1861, Lee was offered command of the Union army. He declined. On April 20 he offered his services to the Confederate States army. He could not turn on his native state of Virginia.

Lee was a gentleman on the battlefield. His men admired him and followed his leadership. He challenged and defeated superior Union forces. It was the manpower shortage, not inadequate leadership, that defeated the South.

Lee surrendered his army to Grant to avoid further unnecessary bloodshed. He had seen too many of his men die. He met with General Grant and surrendered. The time had come to stop fighting and go home.

Lee died on October 12, 1870.

Facing page: Union General Ulysses S. Grant.

Union General William
Tecumseh Sherman.

Another dynamic Union leader was William Tecumseh Sherman. He directed much of the war effort along the Mississippi River. In the spring of 1864, he began the campaign to capture Atlanta. Two months later, he led an army of 50,000 veterans in a destructive march from Atlanta to the sea.

Sherman remained in the army after the war was over. He died in 1891.

The last great leader to mention here is Thomas Stonewall Jackson. He was a good friend of Robert E. Lee. Jackson was daring and clever.

Jackson picked up the nickname of Stonewall from a soldier who saw him during the heat of battle. The soldier said that Jackson looked like a stone wall. He gave encouragement to his men during the battles.

Jackson was mortally wounded by his own troops when they mistook him for a Northern soldier. He died May 10, 1863. Jackson's death was a great loss for Robert E. Lee.

These are only four of the many outstanding leaders of the Civil War. All were devoted men who sincerely believed in their cause.

Confederate General
Stonewall Jackson.

Confederate General Robert E. Lee.

"Drummer" Jackson, of the 79th U.S. Colored Troops.

CHAPTER 2

THE SOLDIERS

When the war began in 1861, men were anxious to be a part of the campaign. They volunteered and joined the various state units. These new soldiers were called green recruits. Foot soldiers made up 80 percent of the fighting force in the Union army.

The average soldier for both the North and the South was between the ages of 18 and 29. His average height was 5-feet, 8-inches (1.7 m), and his weight was around 143 pounds (65 kg).

Drummer boys signed up as young as age nine. (More than 100,000 soldiers in the Union were not yet 15 years of age.) These boys were often called musicians because they not only played the drums, they were also fife players. Soldiers listened for the drum and the fife and often knew when to advance and when to retreat by the beat.

When these young men were not beating time to marches and drills, they were called on to do various tasks. They carried water and stretchers. They helped the cooks and even sharpened the surgeon's instruments. Sometimes they were called on to help with amputations. These boys were often very brave, and sometimes ended up fighting with the regular troops. Some were killed. It always seemed a bit sadder when a drummer boy died.

The soldiers represented all trades. There were farmers as well as business owners. Professional men volunteered. Doctors (called surgeons) and blacksmiths were always needed. Cooks and wagon masters were important to the regiments.

The daily rations for a Union soldier was 20 ounces of salt beef or 12 ounces of salt pork, more than a pound of flour, and a vegetable (usually beans). Coffee, salt, vinegar, and sugar were also provided. The men seldom received fresh meat or vegetables. The meat had to be salted in pickling brine so it could be preserved for two years in any kind of weather. Before the meat was prepared, it was soaked in water. This process removed much of the salt. However, it also did away with many vitamins. When the men were in the field, they often ate hardtack. This was a very hard biscuit. It often contained maggots and weevils. The men had to soak it in water or dip it into their coffee. Often they toasted it to kill the bugs.

It was impossible for the men to have clean living conditions. They were housed in huge tents. Twenty soldiers could sleep in one tent. When the weather was rainy, roads and paths were muddy. When it was hot and dry, dust choked the men.

The bathroom was nothing but a long trench. A new trench was dug every few days and the old one was covered with dirt. It was not unusual for 5,000 soldiers to be living together. Garbage was a big

A log hut company kitchen.

Thomas Taylor, a Confederate who served with the Louisiana Infantry.

problem. It was piled up in big mounds. As it rotted it attracted flies and mosquitoes. The smell alone should have kept the enemy away.

Few battles occurred during the winter months. This time was spent in training. Men drilled, even when snow was on the ground.

Union soldiers at rest after drilling.

It must be remembered that there were no airplanes, no radios, no telephones, and no automobiles. The telegraph had been invented, but it was not always where the men were located, and it did not always work. Information about troop movements was carried to headquarters and to Washington on foot or on horseback.

The bugler was an important person to the soldier. He woke everyone up each morning. In the summer, the men heard the bugle at 5:00 a.m. In the winter, they were permitted to sleep one hour longer. They went to bed at nine in the evening.

Between these times, the soldiers marched and drilled, often for 10 hours a day. They also had to build roads, dig trenches, take care of their horses, chop wood, wash their clothes, and write letters home.

A soldier's chance of dying in combat was 1 in 65. However, his chance of being wounded was 1 in 10. Disease killed many soldiers, for there was a 1 in 13 chance of dying from dysentery, malaria, or typhoid fever.

Sometimes the men were bored. They trained and drilled often, but during the quiet hours and rainy days they thought of home and of their families.

Soldiers became homesick. Sometimes they were very scared. They understood that big battles meant that many would probably be killed. Bullets often mowed down front lines. The men had to be brave.

During the 10 years before the Civil War, over two million immigrants came to the United States from Europe. They had little or no money, and needed work to live. There was no work for them in the South, where everything was done by slave labor, so they settled in the North and East. When the war began, many immigrants volunteered to go into battle. Often they formed their own regiments. The largest group of immigrants in the North was made up of Germans. The Irish were well represented as well. The 39th New York Regiment included many nationalities. There were Hungarian, Spanish, Italian, French, English, and German recruits.

Chaplain conducting mass for the 69th New York State Militia encamped at Fort Corcoran, Washington, D.C., 1861.

The American Indian also played an important role in the war. On the battlefield they were excellent fighters. Some fought with only bows and arrows, tomahawks and war clubs. Cherokee leader Stand Watie reached the rank of brigadier general. He did not surrender his troops until a month after other Southern forces had laid down their arms.

Black soldiers became very important to the war efforts in both the North and the South. Frederick Douglass, a black leader of the time, went to President Lincoln and requested that blacks become Union soldiers. With the signing of the Emancipation Proclamation on New Year's Day in 1863, slavery officially ended. Now the North encouraged the formation of black regiments.

In the beginning, the black soldier was used in less than desirable jobs. He was often called on to bury the dead. He also carried stretchers. Sometimes he helped the surgeons and carried the amputated legs and arms away.

Many black regiments were formed, and these soldiers fought bravely. Over 180,000 black recruits served in the Union army.

The first black regiment to enter into combat was the 54th Massachusetts. These soldiers led the Union charge on Fort Wagner,

near Charleston Harbor, on July 18, 1863. More than half of the regiment was killed or wounded, including the leader, Colonel Robert Gould Shaw. The black soldiers gained the fort's main entrance, and their heroism was much publicized. It brought a change in the public perception of black soldiers. After that, black regiments

A band with the Fourth Michigan Infantry.

In September 1996, Alvin Batiste, a re-enactor in the 54th Massachusetts Infantry Regiment, pauses during a ceremony at Arlington National Cemetery in Arlington, VA, celebrating the African-American Civil War Memorial.

were instrumental in many of the late Union campaigns. This was especially so at Petersburg, Richmond, and Sherman's march to the sea.

The South did not use black troops until March 1865. In Richmond, 300,000 black men rushed to enlist in an all-black unit. They were ready to go to battle when the war ended in April.

CHAPTER 3

THE ROLES OF WOMEN DURING THE CIVIL WAR

Being a girl or woman during the Civil War meant many changes. In the early days of the war, it seemed to be more of an inconvenience. After all, the war was supposed to last only three months. Mothers had sadly said good-byes to their sons. Wives had kissed their husbands, expecting to see them shortly. Little children waved as their fathers went away. No one expected these men to be injured, much less killed. After all, the first battle had produced only one casualty—a Confederate horse.

Suddenly, these same men who had been excited and anxious to fight for their cause were now returning home on stretchers. The women often went from being hostesses to nurses. For women of the plantations in the South, this was often more difficult. Many were pampered by their husbands and cared for by slave labor. Worse yet was news that a loved one had been killed.

The Southern city of Richmond, Virginia, felt the impact of real war for the first time in June 1862. Confederate forces had pushed the Union troops back, but thousands of Confederate soldiers were killed or injured. One Southern lady reported, "Almost every house in the city became a private hospital and almost every woman a nurse."

Refugees leaving the old homestead.

In April 1861, President Lincoln made a call for volunteers for the Union army. Many men from farms and rural communities responded. The women often took up their husband's work. One lady named Elizabeth Thorn was a resident in Gettysburg, Pennsylvania. Her husband, Peter, had been the caretaker of the Evergreen Cemetery. When he joined the Union army, Elizabeth assumed his job. She even helped bury 105 soldiers.

Women also had to take care of financial matters. For many this was something new. Women on the farms also did the chores that needed to be done. It was a great hardship.

It was especially difficult for the ladies of the South. Many slaves left when they received their freedom through the Emancipation Proclamation. With little help, the mistress of the plantation found herself doing jobs she had previously shunned. She made decisions on matters that, before the war, she had known nothing about.

Wives wrote letters of encouragement, especially during the early days. However, as the war dragged on, they often pleaded with their husbands to come home. One lady told her husband all about the crops and animals. Then she said, "I want you to come home, for I want to see you so bad I don't know what to do." It was lonely at home as well as on the battlefield.

The war was fought almost entirely on Southern soil. Cities like Atlanta and Richmond were devastated. Nearly 60 percent of the Southern farms were destroyed during the last year. Most of the livestock was killed. Before the war, Southern agriculture had centered on tobacco and cotton. After the war, even those crops became difficult to raise.

In the North, the Civil War helped manufacturers who produced materials necessary to the war effort. Often the women worked long hours. Then they had to go home and do all the necessary home duties.

Not being on the battlefield did not guarantee safety. The only civilian killed at the Battle of Gettysburg was a lady. Mary Virginia "Jennie" Wade was in her sister's kitchen bent over her wooden dough trough. She was in the process of making biscuits for Union soldiers when a bullet struck her in the back. In her pocket was the picture of her fiancé. He had been killed two weeks earlier.

During battles, many women acted as nurses. They tried to make the injured men as comfortable as possible. They often offered water to fallen soldiers. Many of the women carried a feeding cup that had a spout. The wounded man could drink water or broth from this cup without spilling the contents. Sometimes they would write letters home for the sick and dying men.

Clara Barton was a woman who made a big difference to the fighting men. It all started when she helped nurse the wounded who

Clara Barton, the "Angel of the Battlefield."

were brought back to the hospitals in Washington, D.C. The soldiers' stories made her realize the desperate needs of the men who had been wounded and left on the battlefield.

Earlier Clara Barton had been a teacher in Massachusetts. Now, as she worked among the soldiers, she was surprised to recognize some of the men. They had been her students. As a volunteer she fed them and helped them in any way possible. She often assisted the regular nurses. She was caring and compassionate.

Soon Clara realized that she was needed more in another place— on the battlefield. She knew about the slow wagons that carried the wounded to the closest railway. She had heard how the men often bled to death because their wounds had not been dressed properly. Others had died on the battlefield, not of their wounds alone, but of thirst and exposure. Clara was determined to get permission to go to the wounded men.

She took her cause to Washington, D.C. Finally, she was permitted to go to the front with the Army of the Potomac. Here she often helped the doctors during the battles, and saw piles of arms and legs that had been amputated. She seemed to be everywhere at once. The soldiers called her the "Angel of the Battlefield."

After the Civil War, she received letters from wives and mothers asking her to help locate their loved ones. She was especially helpful at Andersonville prison. In all, she tracked 22,000 soldiers, and was able to notify their families. Clara Barton went on to establish the American Red Cross in 1881. She died in 1912.

CHAPTER 4

CARING FOR THE SICK AND WOUNDED

Hundreds of thousands of sick and wounded soldiers were casualties of the Civil War. Many patients died and others suffered enormously. Medical knowledge of the 1860s was not like today. There were no antiseptics and sterile dressings like we have now. In fact, even doctors did not recognize the importance of hygiene and sanitation.

When a soldier was wounded on the battlefield, he often had to wait until the battle was over before he could be helped. When possible, a sort of horse-drawn ambulance carried him to the medical personnel. Tents were set up as near the center of battle as possible. Here doctors placed a dressing on the wound as a temporary treatment. He was then sent to the rear of the line, where the field hospital was located. Many men bled to death in this process. The bumpy ride caused severe pain, and often the men screamed with each jolt.

Ward in the Carver General Hospital, Washington, D.C.

Wounded soldiers wait their turn at an army field hospital.

At the field hospital, major operations were performed. Here is where the amputations took place. Mangled arms and legs were cut off, sometimes without anesthesia. When anesthetic was available it was chloroform, but some surgeons preferred to operate without it. Chloroform deadened the nerves slightly and made the patient drowsy. The surroundings were often filthy. The surgeons, with their dirty hands, used instruments that may or may not have been wiped off between operations. They did not know about infections. They assumed the wounds would become inflamed and that this was a part of the healing process. Many men died as a result of these infections. If a soldier was shot in the stomach or chest, he usually died from his wound because of the infection. There was no penicillin.

Throughout the war, the Union employed 10,000 surgeons. The Confederacy had about 4,000. Since they often worked so near the front lines, they heard and saw the bullets and cannon balls. During the war 40 surgeons were killed and 73 wounded while attending to their duties on the battlefield.

On the Confederate side, where medical supplies and people were even less adequate, 18 percent of the wounded died from their wounds. On the Union side, 14 percent died from their wounds.

As the war progressed, more hospitals were built. The Confederates at Richmond built Chimborazo, the largest military hospital in the world at that time. By the end of the war, it had 150 wards, capable of housing a total of 4,500 patients. In all, 76,000 men were admitted.

During major battles, many homes became temporary hospitals. Civilians played a major role in nursing the sick and wounded men back to health.

Chaplains were always near the hospitals and the battlefields. They not only aided in caring for the sick in camp and on the march, but also were helpful on the battlefield. They often administered last rights to dying men. They prayed for the soldiers before and during the battles. They stood ready to give encouragement to the men.

Medical instruments of a Civil War surgeon, including a large bone saw used in amputations.

CHAPTER 5

OTHER HELPERS DURING THE WAR

Both the Union and Confederacy made full use of the existing civilian telegraph networks at the start of the war. The North laid 15,000 extra miles of wire between 1861 and 1865. The department in charge was known as the U.S. Military Telegraph Corps. The workers were civilians who reported to the Secretary of War, Edwin M. Stanton. Battery wagons supplied the necessary power for the federal field telegraph operators to send their messages. These wagons were a part of the entire troop movement.

A member of the U.S. Military Telegraph Corps cuts a telegraph wire.

Reporters and photographers with the *New York Herald.*

News reporters were also important. The war was big news, both in the United States and in foreign countries. These journalists had no official status. They simply reported what they saw and often drew pictures of the battles. The public was always anxious to know the latest happenings, so there was a big demand for war news. Soldiers on both sides looked forward to the newspapers because they kept them in touch with what was happening at home. They received their papers either through the mail or from vendors who came into camp.

After the war was over, many journalists went broke. There was no longer a demand for their pictures or drawings. Often their glass plates, which contained the pictures, were sold to greenhouse owners. As the sun beat through the glass, the pictures faded and were soon lost. As a result, many battle scenes are not available. The images and pictures that still exist help us to understand the Civil War a little bit more clearly.

When the war was finally over, brothers came together again. Families were reunited, but life was different. Boys had become men. They had seen life and they had seen death. Many had performed brave acts and helped fellow soldiers.

Three and a half million men had gone to war. Six hundred and twenty thousand of these men died. But the country was now together. It was stronger. The states began to reunite. All that death and pain was a terrible price to pay, but we were finally one country. We were again the United States of America.

A group of Union soldiers.

INTERNET SITES

Civil War Forum
AOL keyword: Civil War

This comprehensive site on America Online is a great place to start learning more about the Civil War. The forum is divided into four main groups. In the "Mason-Dixon Line Chat Room" you can interact with fellow Civil War buffs. The "Civil War Information Center" is especially good for historians and reenactors, and includes help with tracking down your Civil War ancestors. The "Civil War Archive" is full of downloadable text and graphic files, including old photos from the National Archives. When you're ready for more in-depth information, the "Civil War Internet" group provides many links to other sites.

The United States Civil War Center
http://www.cwc.lsu.edu/civlink.htm

This is a very extensive index of Civil War information available on the Internet, including archives and special collections, biographies, famous battlefields, books and films, maps, newspapers, and just about everything you would want to find on the Civil War. The site currently has over 1,800 web links.

These sites are subject to change. Go to your favorite search engine and type in "Civil War" for more sites.

PASS IT ON

Civil War buffs: educate readers around the country by passing on interesting information you've learned about the Civil War. Maybe your family visited a famous Civil War battle site, or you've taken part in a reenactment. Who's your favorite historical figure from the Civil War? We want to hear from you!

To get posted on the ABDO & Daughters website, E-mail us at "History@abdopub.com"

Visit the ABDO & Daughters website at www.abdopub.com

GLOSSARY

Advance
Go forward into battle.

Amputate
To cut off.

Angel of the Battlefield
Name given to Clara Barton.

Army of the Potomac
Primary army of the Union.

Confederate Army
Southern army.

Dysentery
Disease of the intestines producing diarrhea.

Emancipation Proclamation
A proclamation by President Lincoln stating that from January 1, 1863, all slaves in the territory still at war with the Union would be free.

Grant, Ulysses S.
The winning Union general who met with Robert E. Lee at Appomattox Court House, Virginia.

Green Recruits
New army volunteers.

Hardtack
A very hard biscuit.

Jackson
One of the most famous Confederate generals. Best known as Stonewall Jackson.

Lee, Robert E.
Confederate general who surrendered to Grant at Appomattox Court House, Virginia.

Malaria

A disease that causes chills, fever, and sweating.

Rations

Food given to the soldiers.

Retreat

The act of going back, usually used in defeat.

Sherman, William Tecumseh

A famous Union general best known for his "march to the sea" campaign, which helped to win the war for the North.

Union Army

Northern army.

An army blacksmith and forge.

INDEX